# INTO THE COLD

By Jack Gabolinscy

Illustrated by Rochelle Padua

# INTO THE COLD

## LATE

The low clouds and heavy snowfall wrapped the afternoon in a cold, gray blanket. Mom put another log onto the fire and poked the glowing embers. Then she resumed her watch at the window seat. She propped up her broken leg in its cast and placed the cellphone carefully beside her on the seat cushion.

"Dad's very late," she said and began to call his cellphone again. There was no answer.

### First Reading

How well has this introduction told you who the story is about, where the story is set, and when it occurs?

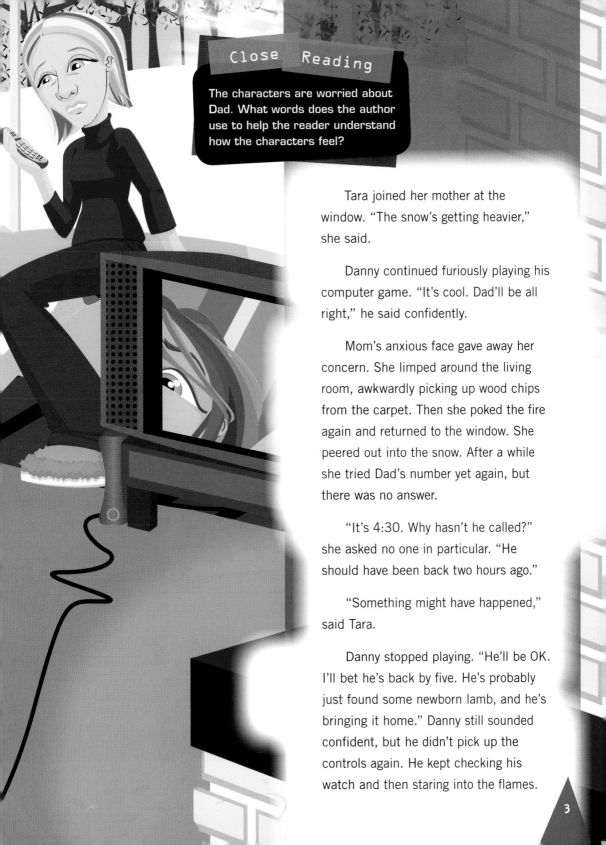

Tara joined her mother at the window. "The snow's getting heavier," she said.

Danny continued furiously playing his computer game. "It's cool. Dad'll be all right," he said confidently.

Mom's anxious face gave away her concern. She limped around the living room, awkwardly picking up wood chips from the carpet. Then she poked the fire again and returned to the window. She peered out into the snow. After a while she tried Dad's number yet again, but there was no answer.

"It's 4:30. Why hasn't he called?" she asked no one in particular. "He should have been back two hours ago."

"Something might have happened," said Tara.

Danny stopped playing. "He'll be OK. I'll bet he's back by five. He's probably just found some newborn lamb, and he's bringing it home." Danny still sounded confident, but he didn't pick up the controls again. He kept checking his watch and then staring into the flames.

At five, Mom tried the cellphone again. Nothing.

She limped to the back door and began pulling on her heavy overcoat. "I'm going to find him," she said.

"Nah, Mom. Don't be silly," said Danny. "You can't go out there, not with your broken leg. I'll go."

"I'm going with you," said Tara.

Mom didn't like it. "It's freezing," she said. "These are dangerous conditions. But you're right. I can't go with my leg in this cast. Both of you will have to go. You'll have to take extreme care. You'd better double up everything."

## "It's freezing"

### First Reading

Do you think Tara and Danny should go out in such dangerous conditions to look for Dad? Why or why not?

Close Reading

What inferences can you make about the characters? Support your answers with details from the text.

... flung away like the snowflakes

First Reading

Who is concerned about not finding Dad? How has this character's attitude changed?

While Danny and Tara changed, Mom hobbled out to the tool shed. She checked the gas tank on the four-wheeler and made sure the first-aid kit and two flashlights were packed.

Danny and Tara came out, layered in their thick clothes.

"Be careful!" ordered Mom. "Don't take any risks! Go down the road, but stop at the bridge. Don't cross it, you hear me! The river will be flooded. Do **not** cross it—no matter what!"

"OK, Mom," agreed Tara. "But we'll find Dad before then, I'm sure."

"What if we don't?" asked Danny.

"You will," insisted his mother.

"But . . ." began Danny. Then he shut up. This wasn't the time to argue.

They put on their helmets and clambered onto the four-wheeler. Tara pressed the starter, and it coughed and grumbled to life.

"The first-aid kit's in the toolbox, too," Mom shouted as they moved off. "Be careful!" she added, but her words were flung away like the snowflakes and lost in the storm.

Close Reading

Explain the meaning of the last sentence. What does the author use to make the message more interesting?

7

Close Reading

What words and phrases does the author use to make this scene meaningful and memorable?

swallowed up in the gloomy grayness

8

# THE SEARCH

Danny and Tara moved down the road, which was swallowed up in the gloomy grayness of the afternoon. In moments, the tracks left behind them by the four-wheeler disappeared. Fears about Dad fizzed like firecrackers in their minds.

The cold nipped at the exposed parts of their faces. Danny shivered and wrapped his arms tightly around Tara's waist. The bright beam of the four-wheeler's headlights barely penetrated the white wall of wind-whipped snowflakes that blocked the way forward. Tara peered anxiously through the windshield. Snow whipped and stung her face, making visibility even more difficult.

"I can't see a thing!" she shouted over her shoulder.

"What?" Danny shouted back.

Tara stopped the bike. "The goggles," she said. "Are they in the toolbox?"

Danny opened the toolbox, took out a flashlight, and came up with two pairs of rubber-framed goggles. He passed a pair to Tara. They were for riding in the dust clouds kicked up behind flocks of sheep, but they would work as well in the snow. They put the goggles on and resettled themselves on the four-wheeler.

Still in low gear, they roared onward once again. The entrance to the race appeared, with the fence posts, like two rows of gray ghosts, on either side.

"Faster," shouted Danny. "Change down a gear."

"It's too sketchy! What if Dad's on the path?" called Tara. "We might crash into him."

For minutes they rumbled on into the storm. Tara honked the horn, loud and long, every few seconds. Danny turned his flashlight on and off. There were no returning signals.

On they rode. At last a dark shadow loomed up on the right. It was the shearing shed. There was a light on. "Look! He's in there!" shouted Danny, tapping Tara on the back and pointing excitedly.

...two rows of gray ghosts

Tara stopped the bike and smiled at him. "He'll be surprised to see us. Mountain Rescue reporting for duty, sir!" She saluted, imitating a movie she had seen.

Danny ran ahead, up the wooden steps. "Dad!" he called, as he raced into the shed.

There was no reply.

He ran into the machine room, yelling again. "Dad? Are you there, Dad?" The only reply was the rattle of the wooden gates and the wind whistling through the rafters.

They searched everywhere. Disappointment, confusion, and the beginnings of fear were creeping into their minds.

"We'll have to go on," said Tara.

"But where would he go?" asked Danny. "Why leave the light on?"

"He must have meant to come back. I guess he didn't make it," she replied.

. . . no reply

What can you infer about
the type of farm this is?
What details help you in
this decision?

...the **bridge** is only a few hundred yards ahead

First    Reading

Why does Danny tell his sister that they are close to the bridge?

14

Back on the bike, they continued their search. It was darker, colder, and gloomier than before. Their sense of adventure disappeared with the last of the dim daylight. The seriousness of what they had to do formed cold, hard knots in their stomachs.

The path twisted and turned up Goat Ridge, then plunged steeply toward the river. The storm wrapped itself closer and colder around them. It howled, like a hungry wolf pack.

Tara shivered, squinted into the gloom, and honked the horn continuously. Danny held on to his sister and shined his flashlight into the gloom. "The bridge is only a few hundred yards ahead," he shouted, but Tara didn't reply.

Close Reading

In the second paragraph, how does the author describe the storm? What does this mean?

First Reading

How does the author describe what happens to the sounds from the horn? What does this tell the reader?

They came to the river and stopped. Tara honked the horn—loud, long blasts that broke up quickly and scattered like confetti on the wind. Danny ran to the bridge. "Where is he?" he shouted.

Tara quickly joined her brother, leaning on the bridge railing, searching the shadows across the river. "What's that?" she yelled, pointing into the river below the bridge.

Danny looked. There was something there. He couldn't tell what. "Come on!" he said and clambered down from the bridge. Tara ran after him. Together, they stomped through the snow, shining their lights into the raging water. What they saw left them hollow with fear. Their father's four-wheeler was almost submerged in the water.

"No!" cried Tara.

Danny didn't say anything. He raised his flashlight beam higher, shifting it farther along the river's edge.

"Look!" said Tara, pointing again. "Do you see that? It looks like his striped jacket, just below the surface."

"It just can't be." Danny echoed Tara's disbelief.

...loud, long blasts

Without thinking, Danny was clambering down the bank, reaching across the rocks and into the black floodwater. The jacket slapped against his hand. He grabbed it and hauled it above the water.

He thought of one word: "No!"

It was their father's jacket. Danny lay across the rocks, unmoving, staring into the darkness of the water. His mind and body were frozen, rigid with the shock of his discovery.

Tara could see the jacket, but she instantly realized something that Danny hadn't.

"Danny!" she screamed down at him. He remained motionless across the rocks.

She knew she had to get him away from the water.

"Danny! Danny!" But he didn't move. He couldn't hear. Tara raced down the riverbank. "Danny!" she screamed.

He turned and looked at her. "He's down there," he said in a hollow voice.

"No! That's not his jacket. Well, it is, but it's the old one he keeps under the seat for a spare."

Tara was right. It was their dad's old jacket. Maybe he wasn't drowned in the submerged four-wheeler after all.

"Come on!" demanded Tara. "Get up out of there. You'll freeze to death!"

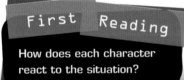

First Reading

**How does each character react to the situation?**

## Close Reading

How does the author show the rise and fall of tension? What is the effect on the reader?

# PAST THE BRIDGE

Tara remembered their mother's orders: *Don't cross the bridge—no matter what*. But that was before. It was different now.

What would her mother do if she were here?

Tara thought only for a moment. "We've got to get you warm and into dry clothes in a hurry," said Tara.

They scrambled back onto the riverbank. Danny was soaked up to his waist, shivering violently. "Shake your legs. Move your hands. Just keep moving."

"What about Dad?" mumbled Danny. "I'm not going home without him!"

"We're not going home," she said. "We're going to the maintenance cabin. It's closer than home."

Danny didn't argue. He was shaking uncontrollably. His fingers and toes were frozen blocks of ice, and pains were shooting through his legs.

"Just keep shaking your legs and moving your hands," said Tara.

**Close Reading**

What inference can you make about Tara from her reaction to the situation?

**First Reading**

Why do you think Danny must keep moving?

... on and on
they went

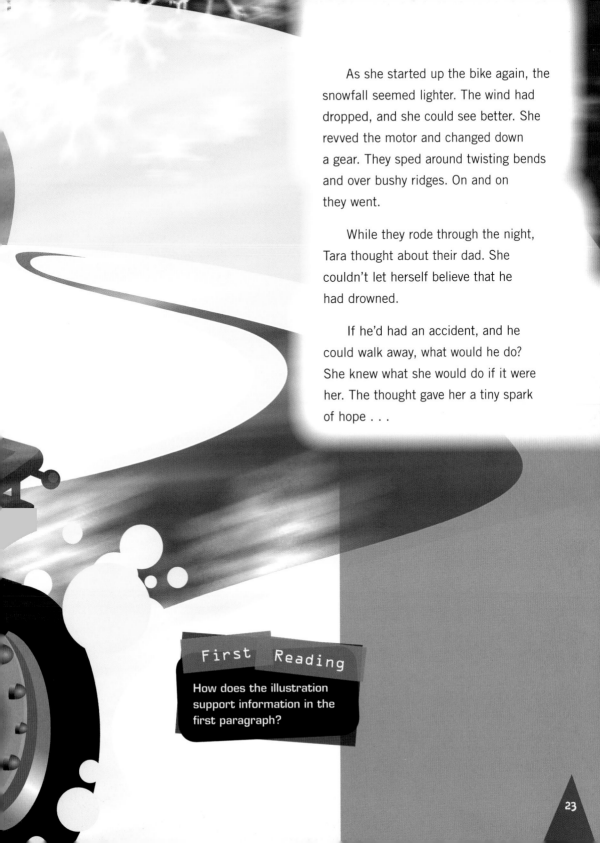

As she started up the bike again, the snowfall seemed lighter. The wind had dropped, and she could see better. She revved the motor and changed down a gear. They sped around twisting bends and over bushy ridges. On and on they went.

While they rode through the night, Tara thought about their dad. She couldn't let herself believe that he had drowned.

If he'd had an accident, and he could walk away, what would he do? She knew what she would do if it were her. The thought gave her a tiny spark of hope . . .

First Reading

How does the illustration support information in the first paragraph?

23

They crossed the last ridge of snow before the cabin and roared down the other side. Tara gripped the handlebars tightly. Hope and fear wrestled in her mind. "Please . . . " she whispered to herself. "Please!"

The cabin appeared suddenly, like a dark shadow squatting among the trees. From its window flickered the dim glow of firelight. Tara smiled. The spark of hope had become a flame. Her heart started to sing.

Tara stopped the bike outside. The cabin door opened . . . it was Dad. He took in the scene in front of him, raced toward the bike, and put his arms around the half-frozen boy smiling groggily up at him.

## First Reading

**Why does Dad race to put his arms around Danny?**

# . . . it was Dad

## Close Reading

What is the problem (or problems) in the story's plot? How is the problem resolved?

# A BONE TO PICK

Dad helped Danny inside, changed his wet clothes, wrapped him in a blanket, and fed him a mug of black coffee. "It's all we've got," he explained gruffly. "This isn't a five-star hotel."

"It's cool," mumbled Danny. "No, I mean it's hot!"

When Danny was comfortable, Dad turned to Tara. "I've got a bone to pick with you," he said in a serious voice. "I thought you were told to stop at the bridge?"

"How did you know?" asked Tara.

"I called your Mom ten minutes after you left," he explained. "My cellphone got wet in the river. I had to dry it out before it would work . . ."

"Well, we've got a bone to pick with you, too," said Tara, laughing.

Danny grinned. "Yeah, great parking skills, Dad!"

# THINK ABOUT
# THE TEXT

Which of the following connections can you make to the settings or characters in *Into the Cold?*

feeling relief

feeling shock

experiencing anxiety

problem solving

# TEXT
## TO SELF

caring for someone

feeling frightened

showing determination

taking responsibility

# TEXT
## TO TEXT

Talk about other texts you have read that have similar features. Compare the texts.

# TEXT
## TO WORLD

Talk about situations in the world that connect to elements in the text.

# Planning a NARRATIVE

## 1   Decide on a plot...

that has an introduction, problems, and a solution. Write them in the order of sequence.

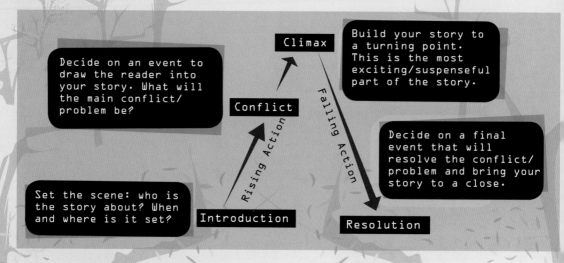

Decide on an event to draw the reader into your story. What will the main conflict/problem be?

Set the scene: who is the story about? When and where is it set?

Climax

Conflict

Rising Action

Introduction

Build your story to a turning point. This is the most exciting/suspenseful part of the story.

Falling Action

Decide on a final event that will resolve the conflict/problem and bring your story to a close.

Resolution

## 2   Think about...

* major and minor characters,
* how they think, feel, and act,
* their physical features, and
* their voice and their way of speaking.

**3** **Decide on the settings.**

Atmosphere/mood

settings

Location

Time

Words that
describe setting

**Don't forget...**

to plan your events
in order of sequence.

# Writing a NARRATIVE

❄ included an introduction that quickly tells the reader . . .
* who the story is about,
* where the story is set, and
* when the story happened?

❄ included a problem (or problems) that makes the reader want to read on to find out how it is solved?

❄ tried to create an emotional response within the reader?

❄ included description and dialogue?

❄ created mood and tension?

❄ included characters, settings, and moods that are connected to create a believable storyline?

Don't forget to revisit your writing. Do you need to change, add, or delete anything to improve your story?